FIRST 15 LESSONS

ELECTRIC GUITAR

Includes Audio & Video Access

T0057716

Video Instructor: Gabriel Andrews

ISBN 978-1-5400-0292-1

PLAYBACK+
Speed • Pitch • Balance • Loop

To access audio, video, and extra content visit:
www.halleonard.com/mylibrary

2674-4636-8995-7644

HAL•LEONARD®
7777 W. BLUEMOUND RD. P.O. BOX 13819 MILWAUKEE, WI 53213

Copyright © 2018 by HAL LEONARD LLC
International Copyright Secured   All Rights Reserved

Visit Hal Leonard Online at
www.halleonard.com

Before we begin actually playing the guitar, we're going to go over a few important non-playing topics, including getting to know the various parts of the guitar, how to tune it up, and how to properly hold it. We'll also learn how to read the guitar tab and chord diagrams used in this book. Let's get started...

GUITAR ANATOMY

The photo below is a Gibson Les Paul electric guitar with each part clearly labeled. Spend some time getting to know each of these components so you can talk with confidence to fellow guitarists about your instrument.

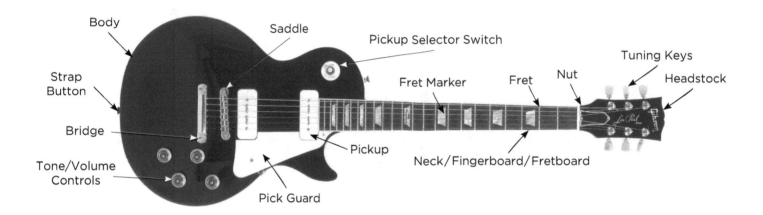

TUNING THE GUITAR

There are many ways to tune your guitar. We will focus on a few of the easiest and cheapest methods...

A free online tuner comes with this book! Simply visit **www.halleonard.com/mylibrary** and enter the code found on page 1 to access it.

You can also purchase relatively inexpensive electronic tuners. Some of today's most popular tuners clip onto the guitar's headstock and "read" the strings' vibrations to determine pitch, while others pick up the pitches via a guitar cable and/or an internal microphone. Many electronic tuners fall in the $10–20 range, making them affordable for most guitarists.

Once you have a tuner at the ready, the next step is tuning each of the six strings. Here are the pitches of the open strings, from lowest/thickest (left) to highest/thinnest (right):

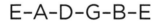

Twisting the tuning keys clockwise will lower the pitch of the strings, while turning them counterclockwise will raise the pitch. As you pluck a string, twist the corresponding tuning key until the tuner's meter matches the desired pitch.

HOLDING THE GUITAR AND PICK

Whether you choose to sit or stand while playing, the main goal is **comfort**. If you experience tension or pain anywhere on your body, then adjustments need to be made. The pictures below illustrate proper sitting and standing posture.

Guitar picks come in several shapes, sizes, and thicknesses. Go to a local music store and try out several until you find one or two that feel comfortable. As a general guideline, thinner picks are better for strumming chords, and thicker picks are better for picking single notes (medium picks fall somewhere in between and might be the best option).

Once you find a pick that you like, place it between the thumb and index finger of your picking hand, allowing the tip to protrude from your fingers enough to cleanly strum/pick through the strings.

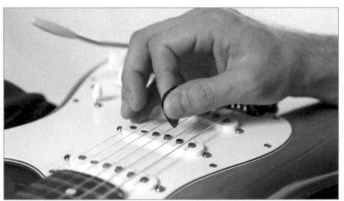

GUITAR TAB AND CHORD FRAMES

In place of standard notation, we're going to use *tab* (short for "tablature")—the go-to music notation for guitar these days—throughout this book. Tab eschews standard notes in favor of numbers, which represent the frets of the guitar. And unlike the standard five-line musical staff, tab is comprised of six horizontal lines, each representing a string on the guitar:

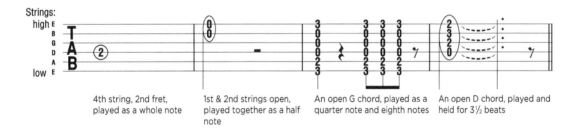

4th string, 2nd fret, played as a whole note | 1st & 2nd strings open, played together as a half note | An open G chord, played as a quarter note and eighth notes | An open D chord, played and held for 3½ beats

In addition to tab, we will be using chord diagrams, also known as chord frames or grids. Diagrams facilitate chord comprehension, especially for visual learners.

Chord frames represent "snapshots" of the guitar neck, as if you were holding it directly in front of you rather than looking down at it while in playing position. The vertical lines represent the six strings, while the horizontal lines indicate frets.

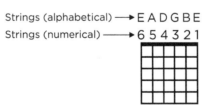

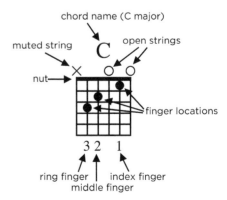

Black dots indicate finger placement, and the numbers below the frames indicate which fingers to use: 1 = index, 2 = middle, 3 = ring, 4 = pinky. When a curved line appears over multiple dots, those strings are to be played with a fret-hand barre. (You'll begin learning about barres in Lesson 2.)

In this lesson, we're going to learn about 4/4 time and how it works with music's most basic rhythms—whole notes, half notes, quarter notes, etc. Then we're going to discuss open power chords and do some actual playing! Let's dig in!

4/4 TIME

The vast majority of music that you'll encounter will be written in 4/4 time, which is why it's also known as "common time." Each number in the fraction, known as the *time signature* (or *meter*), represents a rhythmic component. The top number indicates the number of beats in each *measure*, or *bar* (the space between the short vertical lines in the tab), while the bottom number indicates which type of note receives one beat (2 = half note, 4 = quarter note, and 8 = eighth note). So, in 4/4 time, there are four beats (top number = 4) per measure, and each quarter note (bottom number = 4) receives one beat.

WHOLE NOTES, HALF NOTES, QUARTER NOTES, AND EIGHTH NOTES

A song may be written in 4/4 time, but that doesn't mean we are limited to playing quarter notes exclusively. On the contrary, every rhythm is at our disposal: whole notes, half notes, quarter notes, etc. Let's take a look at those...

As we discussed earlier, there are four beats per measure in 4/4 time, with each quarter note receiving one beat:

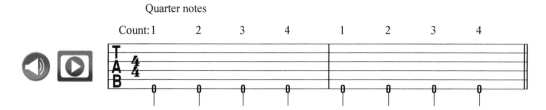

Quarter notes divide the measure into four equal beats, so *half notes* naturally divide the measure in half and therefore receive two beats each. Likewise, a *whole note* occupies the entire measure, so it receives all four beats:

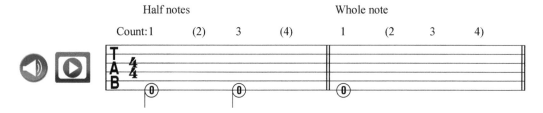

Eighth notes, on the other hand, divide each *beat* in half, with the first note of each eighth-note pair falling on the *downbeat*, and the second note falling on the *upbeat*, or the "and," like so:

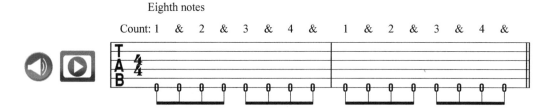

RESTS

Rests are small symbols that tell us when to take a break from playing, and for how long. For every rhythmic note value (half note, quarter note, eighth note, etc.), there is a rest of equal duration. Just as a quarter note equals one beat, a *quarter rest* equals one beat of musical silence. Below is a list of the most common rests, along with their rhythmic values:

TIES AND DOTS

A *tie* is a curved line that connects two notes of the same pitch, indicating that the rhythmic values (i.e., duration) of both notes are to be combined and counted/played as one note. Here are a few examples:

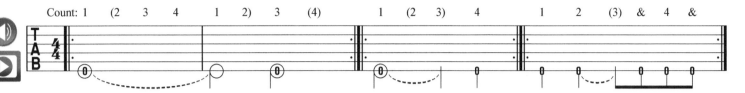

Similar to ties, *dots* are used to increase the rhythmic value of notes. Specifically, a dot increases a note's duration by one half of its original value. For example, the rhythmic value of a dotted half note is three beats (2 + 1), the value of a dotted quarter note is 1-½ beats (1 + ½), etc. The example below shows how dots can be used in place of ties in certain situations:

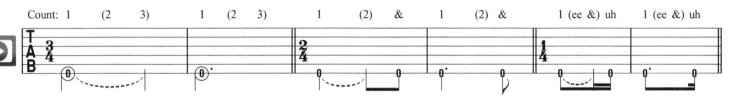

OPEN POWER CHORDS

A *power chord* is a chord comprised of two notes, the root and the 5th, from its relative scale. The *root* is the note that gives the chord its name, and the *5th* is simply the fifth note of the scale. For example, the C major scale (we'll look at this important scale more in-depth in the coming lessons) is comprised of these seven notes: C–D–E–F–G–A–B (1–2–3–4–5–6–7). So, a C power chord, or C5, contains the notes C (root) and G (5th). And when a power chord incorporates an open string or two, we call it an "open" power chord. Here are the most common:

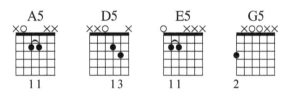

The curved line spanning the dots in the A5 and E5 chords is a *barre*, indicating that you are to lay a finger (the index, in this case) flat across two or more strings to fret the notes. For the G5 chord, allow the underside of your fretting finger to touch string 5, keeping it quiet.

AC/DC's hard rock classic "Dirty Deeds Done Dirt Cheap" contains just about everything we've discussed in this lesson— open power chords, ties, dots, and rests. Despite a little bit of *syncopation*—that is, stressing upbeats (or any beats other than the downbeats)—the rhythms are pretty straightforward. Once you feel comfortable with the chords, try playing along with the original recording using *downstrokes* (⊓) throughout. For the rests, mute the strings with your pick-hand palm, letting it come down gently onto the strings after you strum the chord in the previous measure.

"Dirty Deeds Done Dirt Cheap"

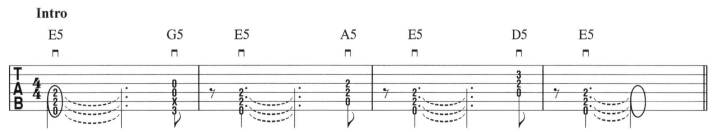

LESSON 3

Now that we've got a handle on open power chords, we're going to take a look at a couple of moveable shapes whose roots are located on string 6. We'll also explore single-note playing for the first time, as well as add a new rhythm to our growing arsenal.

SIXTH-STRING MOVEABLE POWER CHORDS

Like open power chords, the moveable shapes below contain just two different notes: the root and 5th. However, because no open strings are involved, we can move these shapes up and down the neck to play them from any root.

The shapes below are based on the open E5 *voicing* (the order of and distance between the notes of a chord), with the open E string replaced by the fretted sixth string (the root):

The notes on string 4 of these shapes are the roots doubled in a higher register, or *octave*, so the root–5th arrangement is still intact. That said, we can also eliminate the higher-octave root and play these voicings as two-string shapes, like so:

(We can also play two-string shapes of all the open power chords from Lesson 2 as well.)

Below is the main riff to the Kinks' rock classic "You Really Got Me." Here, three-note versions of F5 and G5 power chords are played in a straightforward, driving rhythm. Use downstrokes exclusively and employ your pick-hand palm to gently mute the strings during the rests. The thick bar lines with two dots are *repeat signs*, which tell us to repeat the measures that fall in between them. Note that the first chord comes in before the first full measure; count "1 and 2 and 3 and 4" and play the first chord on the "and" (or upbeat) of beat 4. This is called a *pickup note*.

"You Really Got Me"

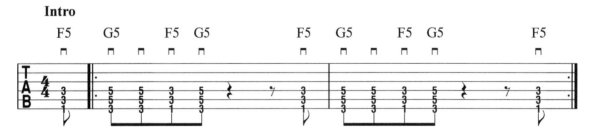

SINGLE-NOTE RIFFS: SIXTH STRING

Single-note playing is a little different than playing chords in that you are focusing your picking on one string at a time, as opposed to targeting anywhere from two to six strings when strumming. In this section, we're going to use a couple of songs—"Runnin' Down a Dream" and "The James Bond Theme"—to get accustomed to picking notes on the low E string.

The main riff from Tom Petty's "Runnin' Down a Dream" starts on an upbeat ("and" of beat 1) with an *upstroke* of the pick (V), alternating upstrokes and downstrokes as you move down the string (this is referred to as *alternate picking*).

"Runnin' Down a Dream"

Intro

16TH NOTES

Before we get to "The James Bond Theme," a quick tutorial on 16th notes is in order. As you recall, eighth notes divide each beat in half, so *16th notes* naturally divide each beat into four equal parts, counted: "1-ee-&-uh, 2-ee-&-uh, 3-ee-&-uh, 4-ee-&-uh," etc. Often 16th notes and eighth notes are grouped together, like so:

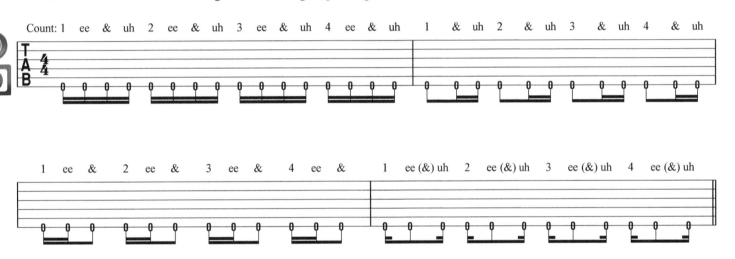

As you can see below, the "James Bond Theme" incorporates some eighth-note/16th-note groupings. Pay close attention to the suggested picking and take it very slow at first. Although alternate picking is the general strategy here, the rhythms do require back-to-back downstrokes or upstrokes at times. And here's how to tackle the different bracketed *endings*: play measures 1–2 three times, but on the third repetition, jump from the end of measure 1 to measure 3 (the third ending).

"James Bond Theme"

Intro

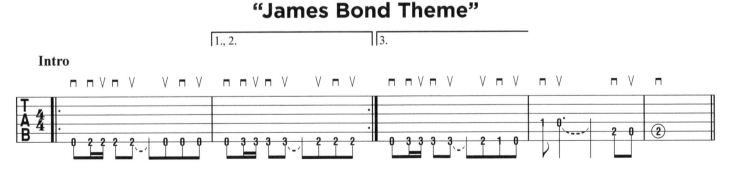

Now that we're familiar with sixth-string moveable power chords, we're going to apply the same shapes to string 5. Then we'll look at how combining sixth- and fifth-string voicings can help us avoid unnecessary fretboard jumps. Lastly, we'll move our single-note studies to string 5 to continue honing our picking chops.

FIFTH-STRING MOVEABLE POWER CHORDS

Like the sixth-string shapes, our fifth-string moveable power chords are also based on an open-position voicing; in this case, the open A5 chord. Below are two- and three-string versions of the A5 chord along with fully-fretted (moveable) shapes:

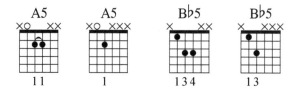

Pat Benatar's guitarist/husband, Neil Giraldo, put three-string shapes to work in Benatar's hard rock classic from the '80s, "Hit Me with Your Best Shot," in a riff that has stood the test of time. Use downstrokes throughout and be sure to apply pick-hand muting during the rests.

"Hit Me with Your Best Shot"

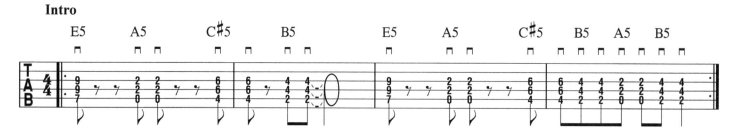

COMBINING SIXTH- AND FIFTH-STRING POWER CHORDS

The benefit of having the same power chord shape on both strings is that you can easily move back and forth between the two. This can be used to your advantage, as it can minimize fretboard jumps.

Check out how Scorpions guitarists Rudolf Schenker and Matthias Jabs jump back and forth between the two forms during the main riff to the group's signature song, "Rock You Like a Hurricane."

"Rock You Like a Hurricane"

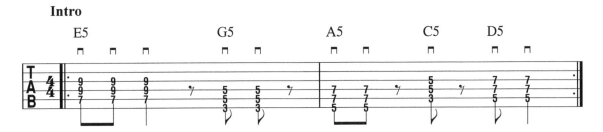

SINGLE-NOTE RIFFS: FIFTH STRING

Playing single-note riffs on string 5 is very much like playing them on string 6. The only real differences are that now you have an adjacent string on both sides—rather than just below—and the string is slightly thinner.

"Breaking the Law" starts on string 5 before shifting to string 6 in measure 3. This riff is pretty straightforward, but be sure to follow the suggested picking pattern. The one tricky spot occurs in measure 4, where you'll need to "roll" your fret hand's ring finger from string 6 to string 5 at the third fret.

"Breaking the Law"

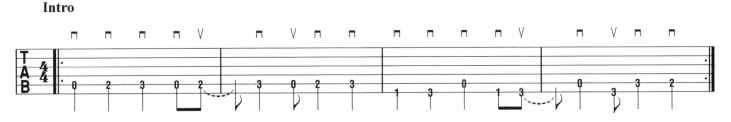

In this lesson, we're going to discuss palm muting and percussive chord muting, a couple of techniques that are frequently used in conjunction with power chords. We're also going to continue our power chord studies, this time taking a look at moveable fourth-string shapes. Then we'll wrap up the lesson with a short tutorial on open-position riffs.

PALM MUTING AND PERCUSSIVE CHORD MUTING

In previous lessons, we've used our right hand to mute strings during rests. *Palm muting* is a similar technique, but instead of dampening the strings completely, it is used to make notes/chords shorter and more defined, particularly when distortion is involved.

Palm muting is a bit of a misnomer because we use the side, or blade, of the pick hand to mute the strings rather than the palm. To execute palm mutes, lay the blade of your pick hand on the strings near the bridge while simultaneously picking them. The farther in from the bridge you move, the more muted the string(s) will be. Let's use Rick Springfield's early-'80s classic "Jessie's Girl" as an exercise. Here, palm mutes are applied to two-string power chords that shift between strings 5 and 6:

"Jessie's Girl"

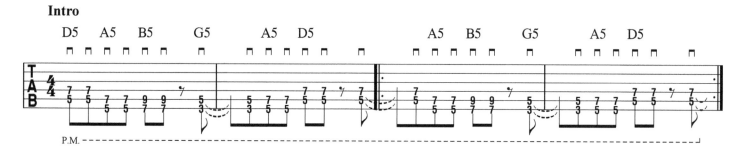

It may have "muting" in its name, but percussive chord muting is quite different from palm muting. Whereas palm muting involves the right hand, *percussive chord muting* is mostly executed with the left hand.

A great example of percussive chord muting is found in Nirvana's breakout hit "Smells Like Teen Spirit," shown below. In this riff, Kurt Cobain intersperses chord mutes between F5, Bb5, Ab5, and Db5 power chords. To perform these mutes, simply release finger pressure from the strings as you strum without taking your fingers completely off the strings. Depending on the speed of the chord changes, you can sometimes lightly lay all four of your fingers flat across the strings to mute them as you strum.

"Smells Like Teen Spirit"

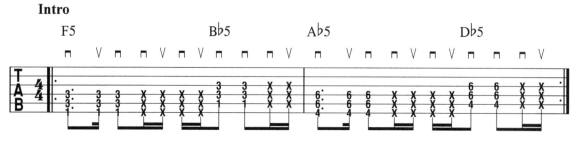

FOURTH-STRING MOVEABLE POWER CHORDS

Although not as common as sixth- and fifth-string power chords, fourth-string shapes can come in handy nevertheless, particularly in those moments when you're looking for a higher-register sound.

When played as a two-string voicing, fourth-string power chords have the same shape as the sixth- and fifth-string versions. However, when a third string is introduced—in this case, string 2—the shape differs a bit from the others due to the guitar's tuning. Fourth-string moveable shapes are based on the open D5 chord, both of which are shown below as two- and three-string voicings:

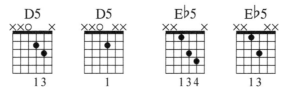

In the main riff to Mötley Crüe's "Looks That Kill," shown below, guitarist Mick Mars plays two-string versions of fourth-string power chords. Notice how he intersperses palm mutes of the open fifth string among A5, G5, and F♯5 power chords.

"Looks That Kill"

Optional: Tune down to match original recording;
(low to high) D-G-C-F-A-D

Intro

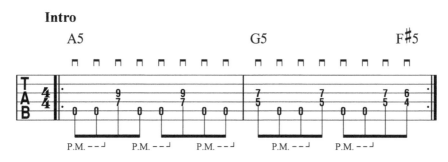

SINGLE-NOTE RIFFS: OPEN POSITION

In this section, we're going to expand our single-note studies from previous lessons to include a few more strings. Below is the main melody to the Ventures' classic instrumental "Walk Don't Run," which moves between strings 5 and 2 and includes several open strings. Be sure to follow the suggested fingerings and picking patterns, which will help to speed up the learning process. That said, if something feels more natural to you, then don't hesitate to change things up a bit.

"Walk Don't Run"

LESSON 6

Through the first five lessons, we've covered just about every type of power chord. Now we're going to shift our focus to three-note chords, or triads. Then we'll wrap up the lesson with a short tutorial on double stops, which are used in both lead and rhythm guitar.

OPEN TRIADS: MAJOR

Whereas power chords are two-note (root–5th) voicings, major chords are comprised of three different notes: the root, 3rd, and 5th of their relative major scales. This is where the term *triad* comes from. Some triad voicings contain more than three notes, but they never contain more than those three *pitches* (some pitches are just doubled in a higher or lower register, or octave). For example, the seven-note A major scale contains the following pitches: A–B–C♯–D–E–F♯–G♯ (1–2–3–4–5–6–7). The root, 3rd, and 5th of A major are A, C♯, and E. Therefore, every A major triad that you encounter will contain those three pitches.

Major triads are used in just about every genre of music—from rock and metal to jazz and country—and sound especially good when played in open position. Let's take a look at the most common open major triads:

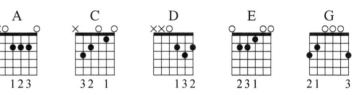

Now let's test drive these chords on a couple of songs. The first chords we're going to use are G, C, and D, and the song is Don McLean's folk classic "American Pie." The rhythm is straight eighth notes, so use alternate (down-up-down-up, etc.) strumming throughout, especially if you're going to play along with the original recording, which is played at a pretty brisk tempo.

"American Pie"

Now let's give our two remaining chords, A and E, a workout. The song we're going to use is Jason Aldean's modern country ballad "The Truth." Below are the first four bars of the chorus section, which feature our two chords, plus D major. The tempo is relatively slow, so use mostly downstrokes when strumming to give the section a little more energy.

"The Truth"

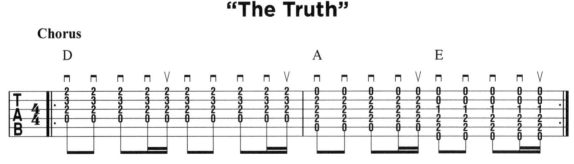

DOUBLE STOPS

Double stops are simply two strings played simultaneously. Sometimes called *dyads*, double stops typically come in two forms: adjacent-string shapes and non-adjacent-string shapes. Let's start by looking at some common adjacent-string shapes.

Here's the G major scale harmonized with double stops:

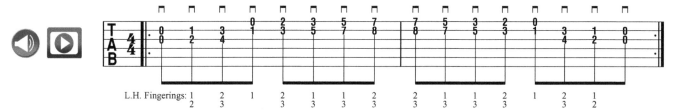

Once you get the shapes under your fingers, practice the exercise with a metronome set at a slow tempo, somewhere around 40 beats per minute (bpm).

A free online metronome comes with this book! Simply visit **www.halleonard.com/mylibrary** and enter the code found on page 1 to access it.

We can do the same type of thing with non-adjacent-string double stops, as seen below using the C major scale. Now the root (in this case, C) is on the higher of the two strings, whereas it was on the bottom string in the previous example. You can strum the double stops with a pick, pluck them with your fingers, or use a combination of your pick and fingers (known as *hybrid picking*). If you strum the dyads, you'll need to use the underside of your middle finger to mute the adjacent string, as well as move the open-strings shape to fret 5 of strings 4 and 2.

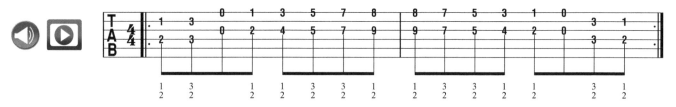

Van Morrison's "Brown Eyed Girl," shown below, is a great example of using adjacent-string double stops to create a fun, catchy riff. Many of the shapes used here are found in the G major scale exercise above, albeit an octave higher.

"Brown Eyed Girl"

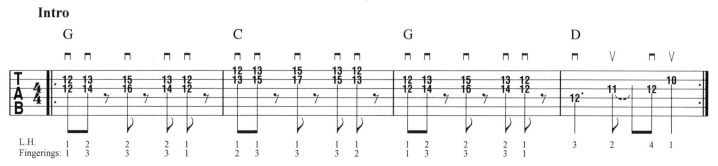

And Deep Purple's "Smoke on the Water" may be the most famous double-stop riff of all time. Here, open-string and fully-fretted dyads are moved up and down strings 3–4 to create a riff for the ages. Use an index-finger barre for all of the fretted double stops.

"Smoke on the Water"

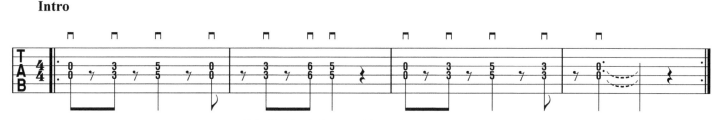

LESSON 7

In this lesson, we're going to continue our triad studies, this time focusing on open minor chords. Then we'll spend some time on arpeggios—a technique that trails only strumming in popularity for playing chords.

OPEN TRIADS: MINOR

If you recall, major triads are three-note chords comprised of the 1st (or root), 3rd, and 5th of their respective major scales, and what makes them "open" is the presence of one or more open strings.

One of the easiest ways to understand minor triads is to compare them to their major counterparts. For example, we know from our previous lesson that an A major triad contains the notes A, C♯, and E. To make this chord minor, all we have to do is lower the 3rd, C♯, a *half step*, or one fret. In our open A triad, the 3rd is located on string 2:

And here are two other minor triads, Dm and Em, shown side by side with their major counterparts:

Now let's put these minor voicings to work in a song. Bill Withers' soulful "Ain't No Sunshine" features all three minor triads presented in this chapter—Am, Dm, and Em—plus an open G major triad. The guitar on the original track was performed fingerstyle, but you can use downstrokes throughout for a similar vibe.

"Ain't No Sunshine"

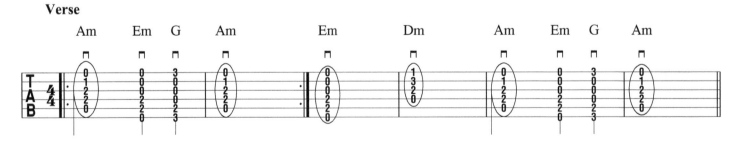

ARPEGGIOS

An *arpeggio* involves playing the notes of a chord individually rather than simultaneously (as with strumming). You can arpeggiate a chord several different ways, but the most basic way is to pick from the chord's lowest note to its highest (ascending) or from highest to lowest (descending).

Let's start with ascending arpeggios using some of the open chords we've just learned. Below is an exercise that features a C–G–Am progression played entirely with ascending arpeggios. Use downstrokes throughout and start with a slow tempo (50–60 bpm). Since we're playing quarter notes, we're unable to play every note of every chord, but that's standard practice. Also, the Am chord is a variation of the open Am we learned earlier in this lesson. Use your pinky for the note on fret 3 of string 1.

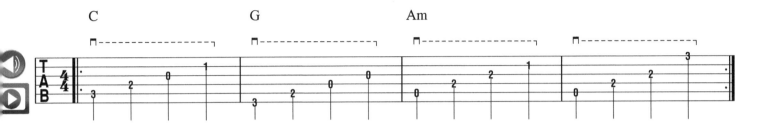

Now let's take that same C–G–Am progression but play it as descending arpeggios. This time, use upstrokes exclusively.

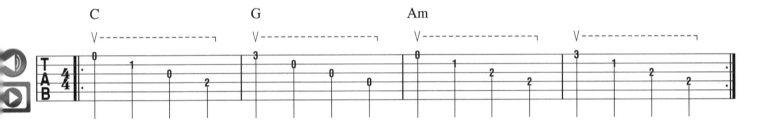

We can create countless arpeggio patterns by simply altering our picking direction on the fly and/or altering which string we choose to play at any given moment. For example, let's take a look at Lynyrd Skynyrd's "Simple Man." In this song, the C, G, and Am chords that we've been working on are played in a pattern that quickly shifts between ascending and descending within each beat. It may look unpredictable, but the pattern is consistent for each chord, so be sure to follow the suggested picking pattern. (If you're going to play along with the original recording, you'll need to tune down a half step: E♭–A♭–D♭–G♭–B♭–E♭, low to high.)

"Simple Man"

Optional: Tune down 1/2 step to match recording;
(low to high): E♭–A♭–D♭–G♭–B♭–E♭

Intro

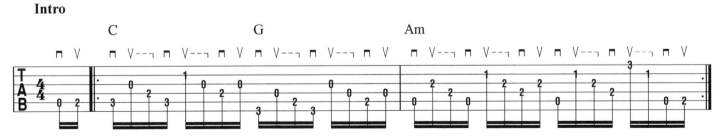

LESSON 8

After spending the previous seven lessons learning various chords and techniques, it's time to apply them to a full song: Green Day's "When I Come Around." This tune features several concepts that we've been working on, including three-note power chords, palm muting, percussive chord muting, arpeggios, and doubles stops, among others. The funny symbol (⌢) over the last chord is a *fermata*, indicating that you should sustain the chord for an extended period of time. (**Note:** If you play with the provided play-along track or original recording, you'll need to tune all of your strings down a half step: Eb–Ab–Db–Gb–Bb–Eb, low to high.)

Demo   Play-Along

"WHEN I COME AROUND"

Optional: Tune down 1/2 step to match recording

Intro

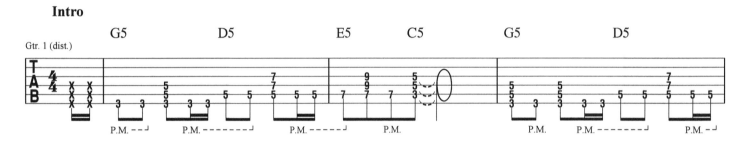

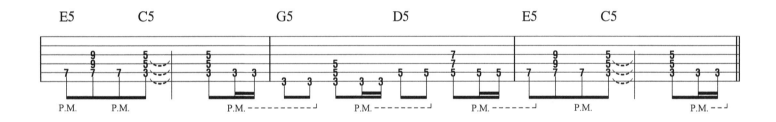

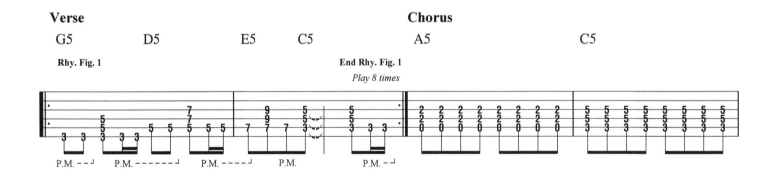

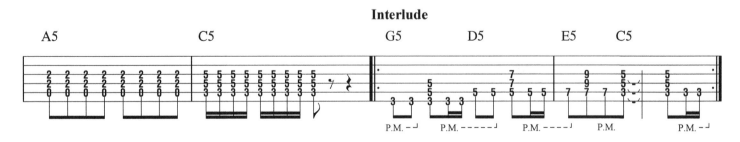

Words by Billie Joe
Music by Green Day
© 1994 WB MUSIC CORP. and GREEN DAZE MUSIC
All Rights Administered by WB MUSIC CORP.
All Rights Reserved   Used by Permission

Verse

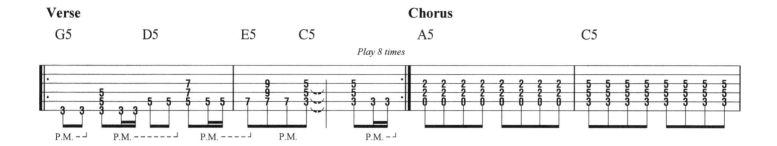

Chorus

Interlude

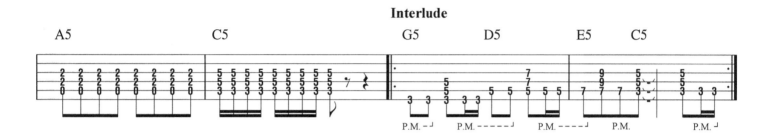

Guitar Solo

Gtr.1: w/ Rhy. Fig. 1 (2 times)

Gtr. 2 (dist.)

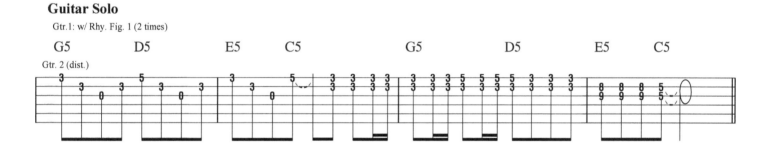

Chorus

Gtr. 2 tacet

Gtr. 1

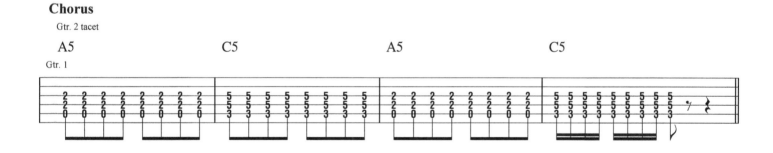

Outro

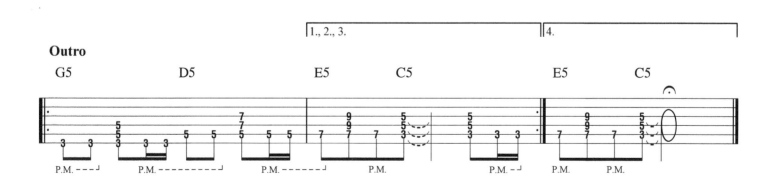

LESSON 9

All of the chords we've learned so far have contained two or three different pitches. In this lesson, we're going to learn dominant seventh chords, which are comprised of four different pitches. We're also going to explore octaves and natural harmonics—two guitar techniques that are used in both rhythm and lead guitar playing.

DOMINANT SEVENTH CHORDS: OPEN POSITION

Dominant seventh chords have both major and minor qualities. This dichotomy is what gives dominant seventh chords their distinctive, bluesy sound.

Like major triads, dominant seventh chords contain a root, major 3rd, and 5th. Unlike major triads, however, they also contain a *minor* 7th, or ♭7th, which is where their minor quality comes from. Therefore, dominant seventh chords can be thought of as major triads with a minor 7th on top. For example, in the key of A major (A–B–C♯–D–E–F♯–G♯), an A triad contains the notes A, C♯, and E (root–3rd–5th), whereas an A dominant seventh (A7) chord contains the notes A, C♯, E, and G♮ (root–3rd–5th–♭7th). Notice that the A major scale contains a G♯ (G sharp), but the A7 chord contains a G♮ (G natural), which is the minor 7th (incidentally, these notes are only a half step, or one fret, apart).

Here are the most common open-position dominant seventh chords:

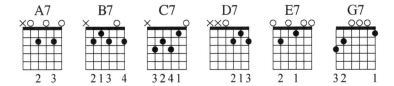

Now let's take one of these chords for a test drive in an actual song. The excerpt below is from the verse section of the Beatles' "Eight Days a Week." After one bar of D major, the progression shifts to E7 for a measure and then finishes up with one bar each of G and D. The eighth notes in this song are "swung," meaning the first note of each eighth-note pair is played longer than the second (a rhythmic feel known as *swing* or *shuffle*). Listen to the original recording to get the feel.

"Eight Days a Week"

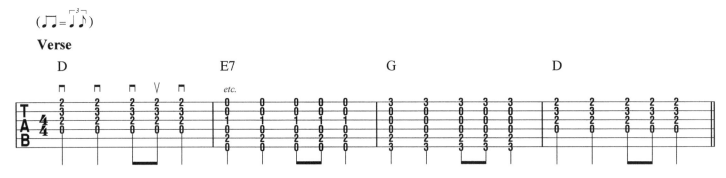

OCTAVES

We briefly discussed octaves earlier in the book; now we're going to play them. This involves playing a note (pitch) in two or more different registers (octaves) simultaneously. Octaves are a great way to beef up a melody, whether in a guitar solo or a rhythm part, and can be voiced several different ways on the guitar. Let's take a look at the most common:

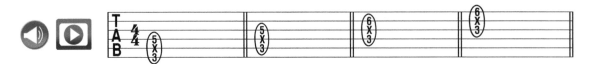

You can pluck them with your fingers, brush them with your thumb (popular with jazz guitarists), or strum them with your pick. If you choose one of the latter two methods, you'll need to use the underside of your fret-hand's index finger to deaden the adjacent string.

Let's take these shapes and work up and down the G major scale (G–A–B–C–D–E–F♯). Play them very slowly at first. The goal is to get comfortable with the shapes, not to see how fast you can play the exercise. Here's a tip: focus your eyes on just the top note of each note pair. This will help you navigate the neck more efficiently and accurately.

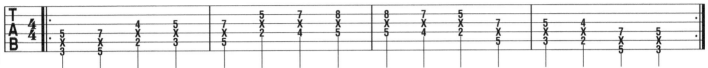

Dave Grohl puts octaves to work in the introduction to the Foo Fighters' hit "Learn to Fly." Here, B, C♯, and D octave shapes are moved up and down strings 5 and 3. If you listen to the original recording, you can hear how the octaves thicken up this melody.

"Learn to Fly"

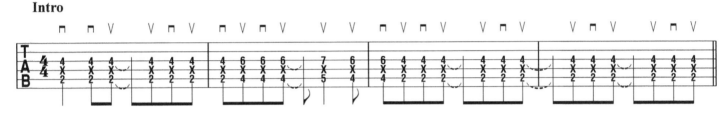

NATURAL HARMONICS

Natural harmonics are created on the guitar by lightly placing a fret-hand finger directly over the wire of one of the frets and, without pressing down onto the fretboard, plucking one or more strings. The result is a shimmery, bell-like sound.

The best locations on the guitar neck for natural harmonics are the 12th, seventh, and fifth frets. These "hot spots" were put to use when Heart recorded their classic track "Barracuda," shown below. After some power-chord chugging, natural harmonics (labeled "Harm.") are played at the 12th and fifth frets:

"Barracuda"

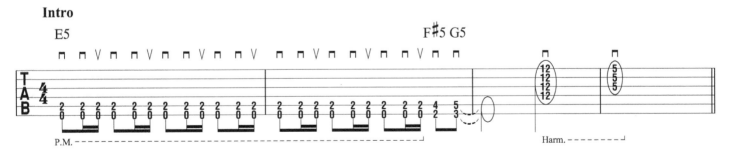

Although the harmonics in "Barracuda" are played in "clusters," they can also be picked as single notes; in fact, arpeggiating harmonics at the 12th, seventh, and/or fifth frets can produce great results:

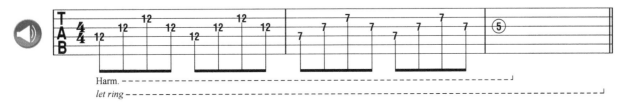

Not all chords fall into the major, minor, or dominant categories, yet some of them are among the most popular for guitarists. We'll focus on a few of these chords—add9, sus2, and sus4—in the first half of this lesson, and then move on to hammer-ons, pull-offs, and slides—important techniques that all guitarists need to eventually master.

ADD9, SUS2, AND SUS4 CHORDS

An *add9 chord* is a major triad with an added 9th. The *9th*, which is also sometimes called the *2nd*, is simply the second note of the chord's relative major scale. For example, the 9th in a Cadd9 chord is D, and the 9th in a Gadd9 chord is A. Let's take a look at some of the most common add9 chords:

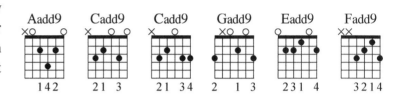

The "sus" in sus2 and sus4 is short for "suspended." A *sus chord* is a triad whose 3rd has been either raised (sus4) or lowered (sus2) one scale degree. Let's run through some of the more popular sus2 and sus4 chords:

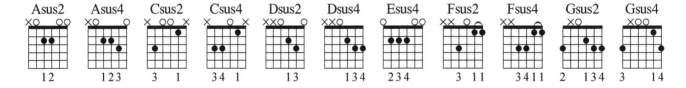

Pete Townshend uses a collection of major, minor, add9, and sus chords in his arpeggiated riff to the Who's "Behind Blue Eyes," shown below. After three straight triads—Em, G, and D—Townshend ornaments his progression with Dsus4, Cadd9, and Asus2 voicings. This song's tempo is pretty fast, but take it slow and steady at first, gradually working up to speed.

"Behind Blue Eyes"

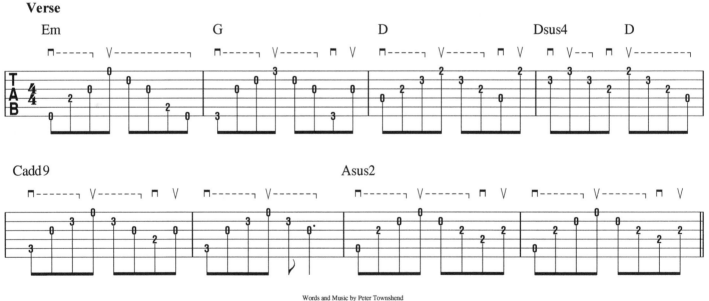

Queen guitarist Brian May employs a pair of sus chords—Dsus4 and Gsus4—in the group's uptempo ditty "Crazy Little Thing Called Love." Like the Beatles' "Eight Days a Week" from Lesson 9, the eighth notes here are swung. And don't overlook the fingerings provided for the G and Gsus4 chords; otherwise, some unnecessarily swift finger shifting will be needed.

"Crazy Little Thing Called Love"

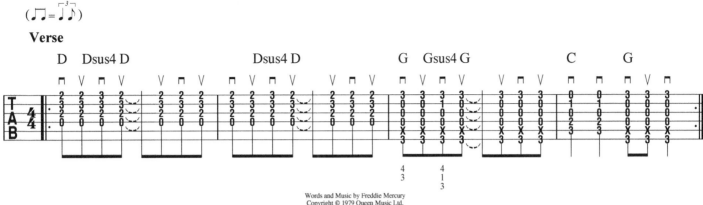

HAMMER-ONS, PULL-OFFS, AND SLIDES

A *hammer-on* involves picking a fretted note (or open string) and then applying another finger to a higher fret on the same string without picking the new note. This "hammering" action causes the second note to sound. The curved line connecting the notes in the tab is called a *slur*. Hammer-ons can be performed one at a time or in a series, like so:

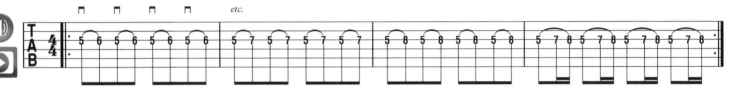

A *pull-off* is the opposite of a hammer-on; it involves picking a fretted note and then "pulling" the finger from the string in a downward motion, thereby sounding a lower fretted note or open string:

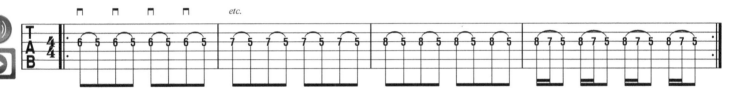

Hammer-ons and pull-offs are not mutually exclusive. On the contrary, you will often see them employed in various combinations, which is the case in Eric Clapton's classic "Layla" riff:

"Layla"

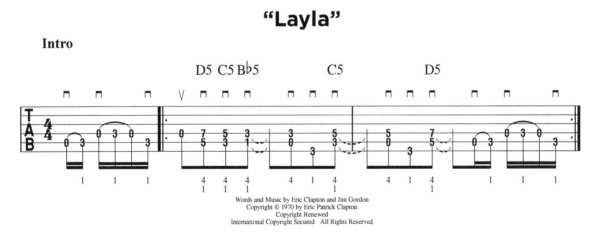

A *slide* is a technique for connecting one note to another. There are two types of slides: legato and shift. A *legato slide* includes a slur and involves picking a note and then sliding up or down the neck to a second note, which is not picked. A *shift slide* is the same as a legato slide, only the second note **is** picked (no slur). Here are some examples of both types:

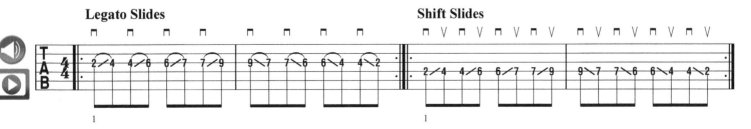

21

LESSON 11

In music, there are four different types of triads—major, minor, augmented, and diminished. We've already covered the first two, so now it's time to cover the others. In the second half of the lesson, we'll shift our focus to string bending and vibrato—two techniques that are vitally important for any lead guitarist.

AUGMENTED AND DIMINISHED CHORDS

Diminished triads differ from minor triads by just one note. Like minor triads, diminished triads contain a minor 3rd, but what differentiates the two chords is the 5th, which is lowered (diminished) a half step in diminished triads. If we take a Dm triad (D–F–A) and lower the 5th, A, a half step, the result is a D° (diminished) triad: D–F–A♭.

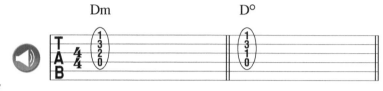

The *augmented* triad is related to the major triad in that they both contain a major 3rd. What differentiates the augmented triad from the major chord, however, is the 5th, which is raised (augmented) a half step in the former. If we take the D major triad (D–F♯–A) and raise the 5th, A, a half step, we get a D+ (augmented) triad: D–F♯–A♯.

Major and minor chords have a stable (consonant) sound and are the chords to which unstable (dissonant) chords, such as augmented and diminished, resolve.

Diminished triads can be tricky to fret, so four-note *diminished seventh* chords are often used instead. Let's take a look at both types:

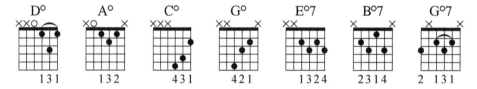

And here are some augmented triads:

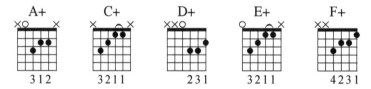

Now let's try out one of these augmented chords in Eddie Money's "Baby Hold On." This progression features just two chords—D and D+ (augmented)—with the latter appearing on the upbeat of beat 4, creating a bit of syncopation in an otherwise straight-ahead rhythm.

"Baby Hold On"

Words and Music by Eddie Money and James Douglas Lyon
Copyright © 1977 (Renewed) by Three Wise Boys Music LLC (BMI)
International Copyright Secured   All Rights Reserved

STRING BENDING AND VIBRATO

String bending is immensely popular in practically every style of music. *String bending* involves "bending" (pushing up or pulling down) a string so that its pitch is raised a predetermined amount. The distance of bends range from a quarter step and half step to a *whole step* (two frets) or more. Once bent, the string can also be "released" to its original pitch. This is known as *bend and release*. Other types of bends include *pre-bends*, *unison bends*, and *oblique bends*, among others.

Before we look at each of these bends, here are some tips:

- **Quarter Step:** use your index finger and pull the string downward (toward the floor) ever so slightly.

- **Half Step**, **Whole Step**, and **Bend and Release:** bend with your ring finger, reinforcing it with your middle and index (essentially bending with all three fingers).

- **Pre-Bend and Release:** using all three fingers, bend the string to pitch, **then** pick it and release it.

- **Unison Bends:** fret the note on string 2 with your index finger, bending string 3 with your ring and middle fingers. The bent note should match the pitch of the fretted one.

- **Oblique Bends:** fret the note on string 2 with your pinky, bending string 3 with your ring, middle, and index fingers.

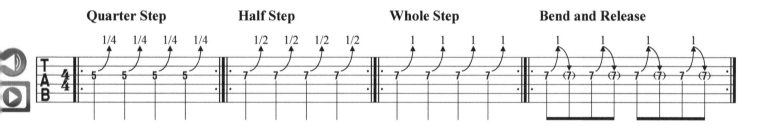

A good way to determine if you are bending the string to its proper pitch is to match the bent pitch to the fretted note located one fret (half step) or two frets (whole step) above the starting point.

Vibrato is a technique that involves rapidly bending and releasing a string slightly with the fret hand. The result is akin to the vibrato you hear in a singer's voice. Vibrato can be applied to one or more notes and is often used in conjunction with string bending.

Let's put some whole-step bends and vibrato into practice by playing the intro melody to Eric Clapton's timeless ballad "Wonderful Tonight":

"Wonderful Tonight"

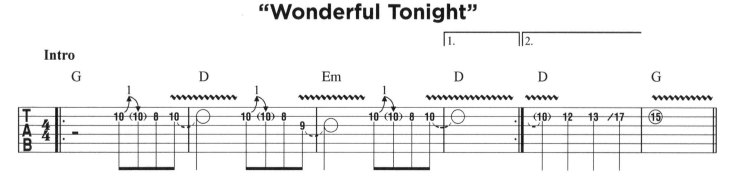

In the previous 11 lessons, we've covered open-position major, minor, augmented, and diminished triads, as well as suspended and add chords. In this lesson, we're going to start moving up the neck and delve into barre chords. Later, we'll continue our single-note studies by learning to play a couple of fully-fretted (no open strings) riffs.

SIXTH-STRING MAJOR AND MINOR BARRE CHORDS

A *barre chord* can essentially refer to any chord that contains a barre, or one finger fretting more than one string. This lesson will focus on one of the most common groups of barre chords: sixth-string major and minor shapes.

The sixth-string major shape is simply the open E major triad moved up the fretboard, with an index-finger barre replacing the open strings. Here are the open E and an F major barre chords side by side:

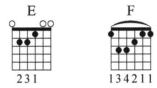

Six-string barres are difficult for beginners, so don't be discouraged if you struggle with the shape at first. To help with this problem, below is an exercise that features a few major shapes played along the fretboard. The chords get their name from the note on the sixth string (G = fret 3, C = fret 8, and D = fret 10). Use a metronome, such as the free online one that comes with this book, and set it to a very slow tempo (40–50 bpm). Don't worry if you miss a beat here or there; the main concern is getting comfortable with the shape and moving it around.

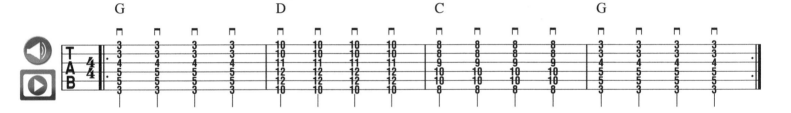

Like the major voicing, the sixth-string minor shape is based on an open-position triad; this time, Em. Here are the Em and Fm chords side by side:

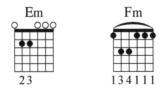

Now let's take the exercise from above and replace the major chords with minor shapes:

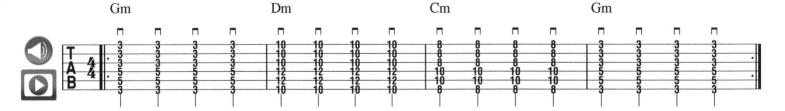

24

Below is an excerpt from Jimi Hendrix's version of Bob Dylan's "All Along the Watchtower," a song that prominently features sixth-string major (A and B) and minor (C#m) barre chords. (**Note:** You'll need to tune down a half step [low to high: Eb–Ab–Db–Gb–Bb–Eb] to play along with the original recording.)

"All Along the Watchtower"

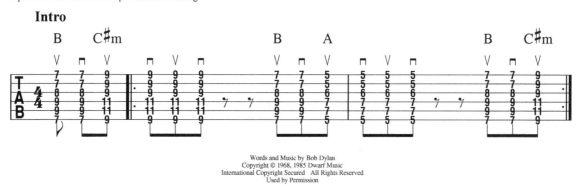

SINGLE-NOTE RIFFS: FULLY FRETTED

We've spent quite a bit of our single-note studies on riffs that incorporate open strings. Now we're going to turn our attention to fully-fretted riffs, which require a bit more fret-hand strength and stamina since open strings are not available to offer any relief.

The first example we're going to play is the main riff to Marilyn Manson's cover of the Eurythmics' "Sweet Dreams (Are Made of This)." This riff gives the index and ring fingers a good workout. Play each note with a downstroke and let them ring out (i.e., don't apply palm muting).

"Sweet Dreams (Are Made of This)"

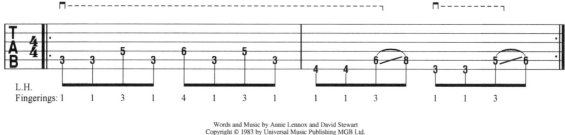

This next riff, taken from Kansas' "Carry on Wayward Son," is a bit trickier. It's played at a faster tempo than "Sweet Dreams," and position shifts are involved. The part that might trip you up the most occurs on beat 1 of measure 2, where you'll need to "roll" your ring finger from string 6 to string 5 (at fret 5), so take it slowly at first, working up to the speed of the original.

"Carry on Wayward Son"

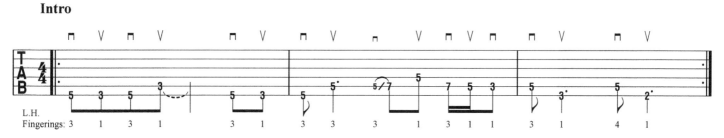

Now that we're familiar with full, six-string barres, it's time to take a look at their fifth-string counterparts. In this lesson, we'll learn the voicings for major and minor barre chords whose roots are located on string 5. Then we'll get our first taste of playing actual scales. Let's go!

FIFTH-STRING MAJOR AND MINOR BARRE CHORDS

Fifth-string barre chords are actually quite different from their six-string counterparts. Whereas the sixth-string major barre chord features an index-finger barre that spans all six strings, the fifth-string major barre chord actually involves a **ring-finger barre**. This shape is the open A chord moved up the fretboard, with the index finger replacing the open A string:

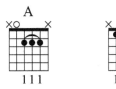

This ring-finger barre will take some time getting used to, as it must be flattened so that you're fretting strings 4–2 simultaneously. Moving your fret-hand thumb to the center of the neck will help facilitate this technique. Once you feel as though you have the voicing under your fingers, give this exercise a try:

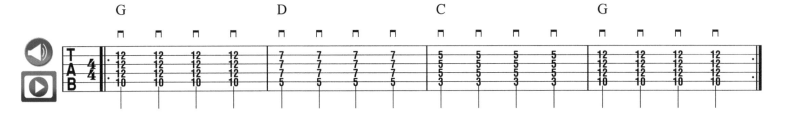

Like the major barre chord, the fifth-string minor barre-chord shape is also based on an open chord; this time, it's the open Am triad:

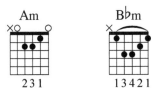

The minor shape is a little easier to voice than the major barre chord, but the index-finger barre, which is responsible for notes on both string 1 and string 5, will still take some practice. Here's an exercise to get you started:

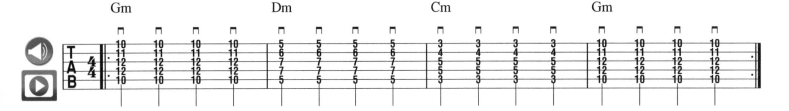

Not let's apply our sixth- and fifth-string barre chords to a song. In the following excerpt from Jack Johnson's "Flake," minor and major shapes are played along strings 5 and 6 in a syncopated rhythm that is somewhat complex—although it's easier to play than it looks. Chord mutes are used as a percussive element, which adds to the complexity. The best way to get a feel for this groove is to listen to and play along with the original recording.

"Flake"

Intro

Dm

F

Bb

F

Words and Music by Jack Johnson
Copyright © 2000 by Bubble Toes Publishing (ASCAP)
All Rights Administered by Universal Music Corp.
All Rights Reserved   Used by Permission

THE MAJOR AND MINOR SCALES

The foundation of Western music is the *major scale* and, to a lesser degree, the *minor scale*. These seven-note scales provide the pitches for the chords that we've been studying and are the note sources for song melodies and guitar solos. In this section, we'll learn common patterns for both scales while, at the same time, practicing our alternate picking.

First up is the major scale, illustrated below in the key of A (A–B–C♯–D–E–F♯–G♯). The scale spans two octaves and is notated in both ascending and descending order. Practice the scale by starting with a downstroke; then switch it up on the second pass and begin with an upstroke.

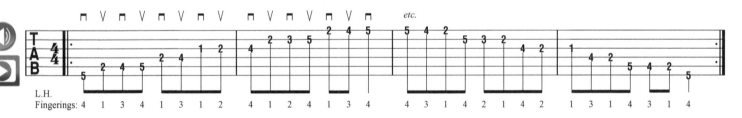

Now let's practice the two-octave A *minor* scale (A–B–C–D–E–F–G). Again, start with a downstroke initially, and then switch to an upstroke on the repeat. The goal is to get comfortable picking in either direction, irrespective of the note. And this goes without saying: practice with a metronome, starting with a tempo in the 40–50 bpm range.

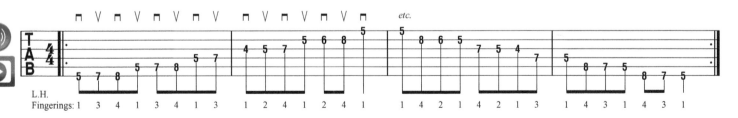

Since no open strings are present in either scale, you can move these patterns up and down the neck to play in other keys. All you need to do is line up the first note of the patterns with the root of the key in which you want to play (A = fret 5, Bb = fret 6, B = fret 7, C = fret 8, etc.).

In Lesson 9, we learned a few dominant seventh voicings in open position. Now, we're going to learn barre-chord versions of these chords, as well as ones for major seventh and minor seventh chords. Then we'll move on to more scale studies, this time focusing on five-note variations (i.e., pentatonic) of the seven-note major and minor scales we learned in Lesson 13.

BARRE CHORDS: MAJOR, MINOR, AND DOMINANT SEVENTHS

As mentioned in Lesson 9, dominant seventh chords are like major triads but with a minor 7th on top. We can think of major seventh and minor seventh chords in a similar fashion. For example, major seventh chords also contain the notes of a major triad but with a **major** 7th on top. In the key of C (C–D–E–F–G–A–B), a dominant seventh chord (C7) contains the notes C, E, G, and B♭ (1–3–5–♭7). A major seventh chord (Cmaj7), however, contains the notes C, E, G, and **B** (1–3–5–7). In the key of C, B♭ is a minor 7th, whereas B is a major 7th.

Similarly, a minor seventh chord contains the notes of a **minor** triad but with a **minor** 7th on top. In the key of C minor (C–D–E♭–F–G–A♭–B♭), a minor seventh chord (Cm7) is comprised of the notes C, E♭, G, and B♭.

Below are some common barre-chord voicings for each of these chord qualities:

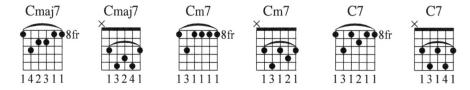

Now let's take these shapes for a test drive on a couple of songs. Our first tune is the Red Hot Chili Peppers' "Under the Bridge." This excerpt, taken from the song's verse, features several major and minor barre chords played on strings 5 and 6. After two repetitions of this four-bar progression, guitarist John Frusciante resolves the section and builds anticipation for the next one with a well-placed Emaj7 chord.

"Under the Bridge"

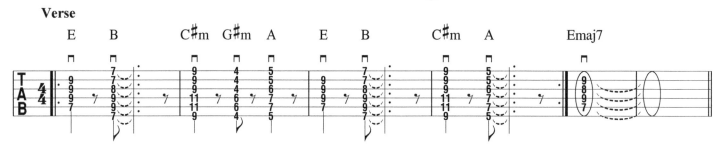

In "Stray Cat Strut," swing cat Brian Setzer walks down string 6 with a semi-chromatic progression featuring both minor seventh (Cm7) and dominant seventh (B♭7, A♭7, and G7) voicings. The eighth notes in this song are swung, so hold the first eighth note of each eighth-note pair a little longer than the second. Also, cut the quarter notes short (i.e., play them staccato).

"Stray Cat Strut"

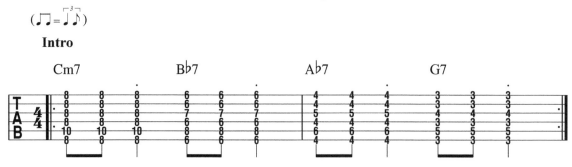

THE PENTATONIC AND BLUES SCALES

Every seven-note major and minor scale has a five-note counterpart, known as the *major pentatonic* and *minor pentatonic* scale, respectively. Pentatonic scales are wildly popular; in fact, guitar players get more mileage out these than their seven-note companions.

The major pentatonic scale is comprised of the first, second, third, fifth, and sixth notes of the major scale. So, in the key of A major (A–B–C♯–D–E–F♯–G♯), the major pentatonic is spelled: A–B–C♯–E–F♯ (1–2–3–5–6). Let's take a look at A major and A major pentatonic side by side:

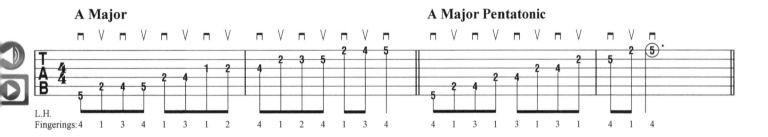

The minor pentatonic scale is built from the first, third, fourth, fifth, and seventh notes of the minor scale. So, in the key of A minor (A–B–C–D–E–F–G), the minor pentatonic is spelled: A–C–D–E–G (1–♭3–4–5–♭7). Let's take a look at A minor and A minor pentatonic side by side:

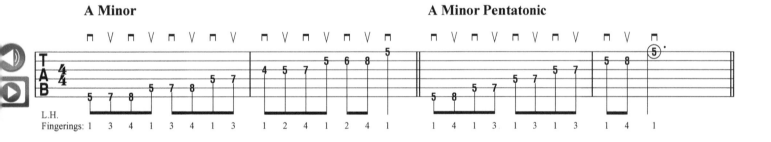

The minor pentatonic scale also has a six-note relative: the blues scale. The *blues scale* contains the same notes as the minor pentatonic scale but has one additional pitch—the ♭5th (pronounced "flat fifth")—which gives the scale additional minor-key heft. In the key of A minor, the ♭5th is E♭, so the A blues scale is spelled: A–C–D–E♭–E–G (1–♭3–4–♭5–5–♭7). Here is the A blues scale in ascending and descending order:

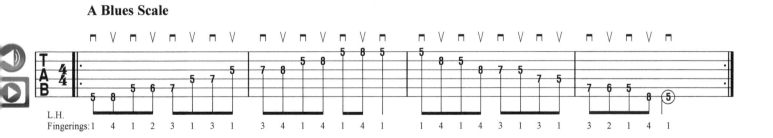

The Who's "I Can't Explain" is going to be our reward for 14 lessons of hard work! Below is the tab for the entire song, including **two** guitar solos. Some of the topics that we've studied—sixth- and fifth-string barre chords, sus chords, pull-offs, slides, double stops, etc.—are found in the arrangement. The tempo is a brisk 141 bpm, so you'll need to spend quite a bit of time working with a metronome at slower tempos before you'll be ready to use the play-along track or the original recording. Good luck!

"I CAN'T EXPLAIN"

Demo   Play-Along

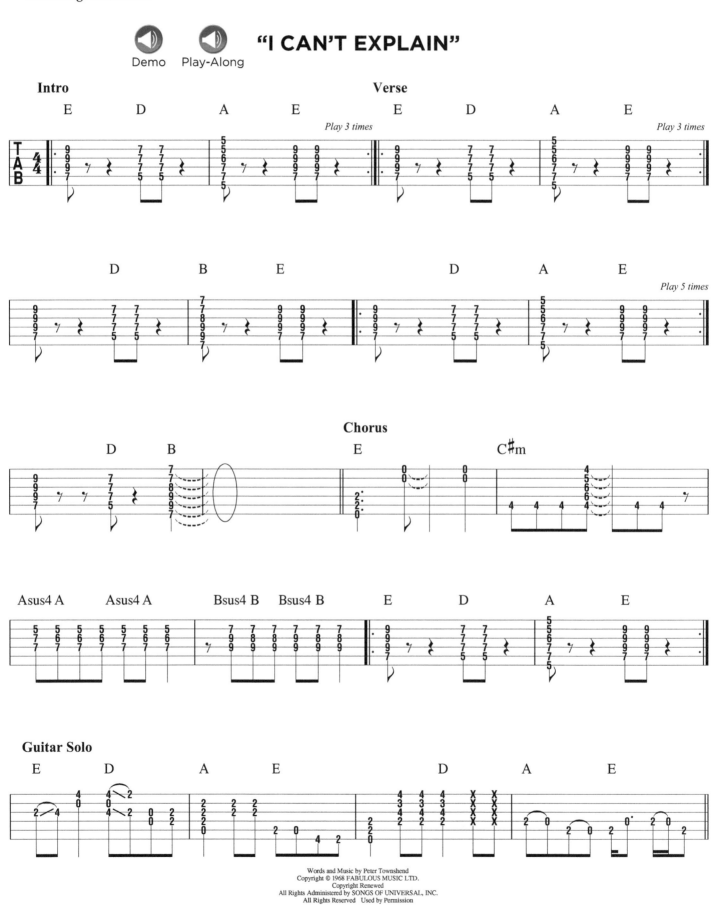

Verse

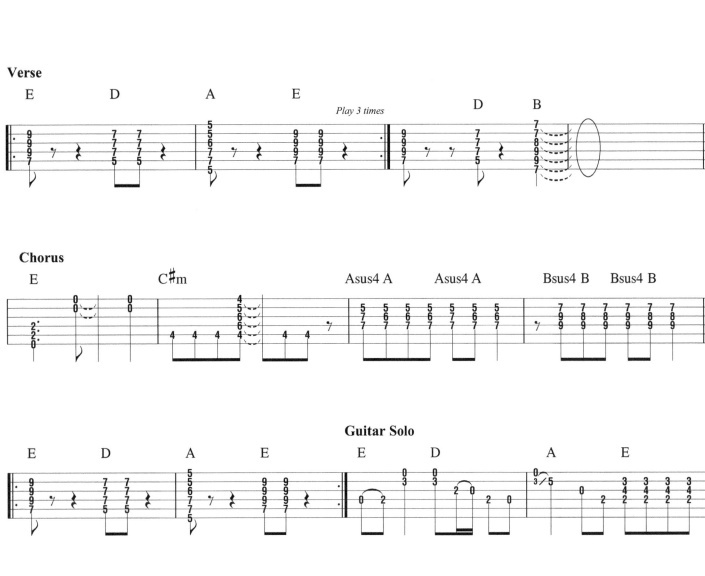

Chorus

Guitar Solo

Outro

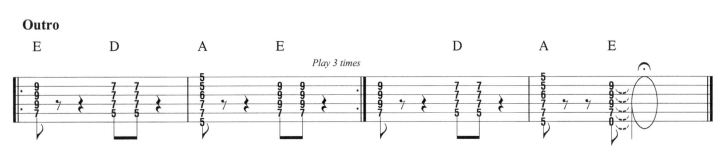

Get Better at Guitar

...with these Great Guitar Instruction Books from Hal Leonard!

101 GUITAR TIPS
INCLUDES TAB

STUFF ALL THE PROS KNOW AND USE

by Adam St. James

This book contains invaluable guidance on everything from scales and music theory to truss rod adjustments, proper recording studio set-ups, and much more.

00695737 Book/Online Audio $16.99

AMAZING PHRASING
INCLUDES TAB

by Tom Kolb

This book/audio pack explores all the main components necessary for crafting well-balanced rhythmic and melodic phrases. It also explains how these phrases are put together to form cohesive solos. The companion audio contains 89 demo tracks, most with full-band backing.

00695583 Book/Online Audio $19.99

ARPEGGIOS FOR THE MODERN GUITARIST
INCLUDES TAB

by Tom Kolb

Using this no-nonsense book with online audio, guitarists will learn to apply and execute all types of arpeggio forms using a variety of techniques, including alternate picking, sweep picking, tapping, string skipping, and legato.

00695862 Book/Online Audio $19.99

BLUES YOU CAN USE

by John Ganapes

This comprehensive source for learning blues guitar is designed to develop both your lead and rhythm playing. Includes: 21 complete solos • blues chords, progressions and riffs • turnarounds • movable scales and soloing techniques • string bending • utilizing the entire fingerboard • and more.

00142420 Book/Online Media..................................$19.99

CONNECTING PENTATONIC PATTERNS
INCLUDES TAB

by Tom Kolb

If you've been finding yourself trapped in the pentatonic box, this book is for you! This hands-on book with online audio offers examples for guitar players of all levels, from beginner to advanced. Study this book faithfully, and soon you'll be soloing all over the neck with the greatest of ease.

00696445 Book/Online Audio $19.99

FRETBOARD MASTERY
INCLUDES TAB

by Troy Stetina

Untangle the mysterious regions of the guitar fretboard and unlock your potential. This book familiarizes you with all the shapes you need to know by applying them in real musical examples, thereby reinforcing and reaffirming your newfound knowledge.

00695331 Book/Online Audio $19.99

GUITAR AEROBICS
INCLUDES TAB

by Troy Nelson

Here is a daily dose of guitar "vitamins" to keep your chops fine tuned! Musical styles include rock, blues, jazz, metal, country, and funk. Techniques taught include alternate picking, arpeggios, sweep picking, string skipping, legato, string bending, and rhythm guitar.

00695946 Book/Online Audio $19.99

GUITAR CLUES
INCLUDES TAB

OPERATION PENTATONIC

by Greg Koch

Whether you're new to improvising or have been doing it for a while, this book/audio pack will provide loads of delicious licks and tricks that you can use right away, from volume swells and chicken pickin' to intervallic and chordal ideas.

00695827 Book/Online Audio $19.99

PAT METHENY – GUITAR ETUDES
INCLUDES TAB

Over the years, in many master classes and workshops around the world, Pat has demonstrated the kind of daily workout he puts himself through. This book includes a collection of 14 guitar etudes he created to help you limber up, improve picking technique and build finger independence.

00696587..$15.99

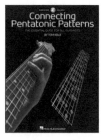

PICTURE CHORD ENCYCLOPEDIA

This comprehensive guitar chord resource for all playing styles and levels features five voicings of 44 chord qualities for all twelve keys – 2,640 chords in all! For each, there is a clearly illustrated chord frame, as well as *an actual photo* of the chord being played!.

00695224..$19.99

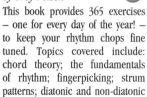

RHYTHM GUITAR 365
INCLUDES TAB

by Troy Nelson

This book provides 365 exercises – one for every day of the year! – to keep your rhythm chops fine tuned. Topics covered include: chord theory; the fundamentals of rhythm; fingerpicking; strum patterns; diatonic and non-diatonic progressions; triads; major and minor keys; and more.

00103627 Book/Online Audio $24.99

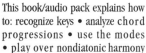

SCALE CHORD RELATIONSHIPS
INCLUDES TAB

by Michael Mueller & Jeff Schroedl

This book/audio pack explains how to: recognize keys • analyze chord progressions • use the modes • play over nondiatonic harmony • use harmonic and melodic minor scales • use symmetrical scales • incorporate exotic scales • and much more!

00695563 Book/Online Audio $14.99

SPEED MECHANICS FOR LEAD GUITAR
INCLUDES TAB

by Troy Stetina

Take your playing to the stratosphere with this advanced lead book which will help you develop speed and precision in today's explosive playing styles. Learn the fastest ways to achieve speed and control, secrets to make your practice time really count, and how to open your ears and make your musical ideas more solid and tangible.

00699323 Book/Online Audio $19.99

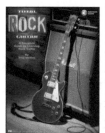

TOTAL ROCK GUITAR
INCLUDES TAB

by Troy Stetina

This comprehensive source for learning rock guitar is designed to develop both lead and rhythm playing. It covers: getting a tone that rocks • open chords, power chords and barre chords • riffs, scales and licks • string bending, strumming, and harmonics • and more.

00695246 Book/Online Audio $19.99

Guitar World Presents STEVE VAI'S GUITAR WORKOUT
INCLUDES TAB

In this book, Steve Vai reveals his path to virtuoso enlightenment with two challenging guitar workouts – one 10-hour and one 30-hour – which include scale and chord exercises, ear training, sight-reading, music theory, and much more.

00119643..$14.99